MONSTER ⚙ MACHINES

TRUCKS

DAVID JEFFERIS

Belitha Press

▼ This eight-wheel truck was specially built for towing wrecked vehicles.

First published in Great Britain in 2001 by Belitha Press Limited, London House, Great Eastern Wharf, Parkgate Road, London SW11 4NQ

Copyright © David Jefferis 2001

Design and editorial production Alpha Communications
Educational advisor Julie Stapleton
Picture research Kay Rowley

ISBN 1 84138 192 6

British Library Cataloguing in Publication Data for this book is available from the British Library.

Printed in Singapore
10 9 8 7 6 5 4 3 2 1

Acknowledgements
We wish to thank the following individuals and organizations for their help and assistance and for supplying material in their collections:
Alpha Archive, Tim Andrew, Caterpillar Inc, George Hall/Code Red, DAF Racing, General Motors Corp, Kenworth Truck Company, Leyland Trucks, HW Lovell & Son, Leyland DAF, Monster Trucks.com, Oshkosh Truck Corp, Pakkar Inc, Peterbilt Motors Company, Quadrant Picture Library/Jeremy Hoare, Samsung Corp, Scania Trucks, Tamiya Inc, The Stock Market, Volvo Truck Corp

Illustrations and diagrams by Ron Jobson, Gavin Page

CONTENTS

⚙ TECH-TALK
Look for the cog and blue box for explanations of technical terms.

👁 EYE-VIEW
Look for the eye and yellow box for eyewitness accounts.

HEAVY HAULERS

Trucks haul most of the world's freight. They carry goods on roads that range from mountain tracks to superhighways.

▲ In 1911 most trucks were built with cabs that were open to wind and weather.

Trucks are made in two basic types. Rigid trucks have a single metal backbone, called the chassis. The cab, engine and wheels are mounted on the chassis. Cargo is carried behind the cab.

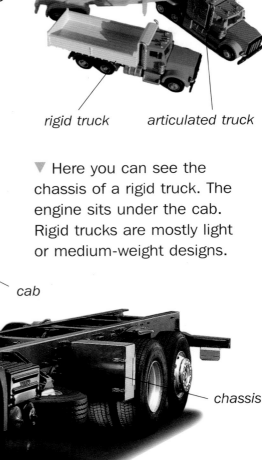

rigid truck   articulated truck

▼ Here you can see the chassis of a rigid truck. The engine sits under the cab. Rigid trucks are mostly light or medium-weight designs.

cab

VOLVO

FM7

chassis

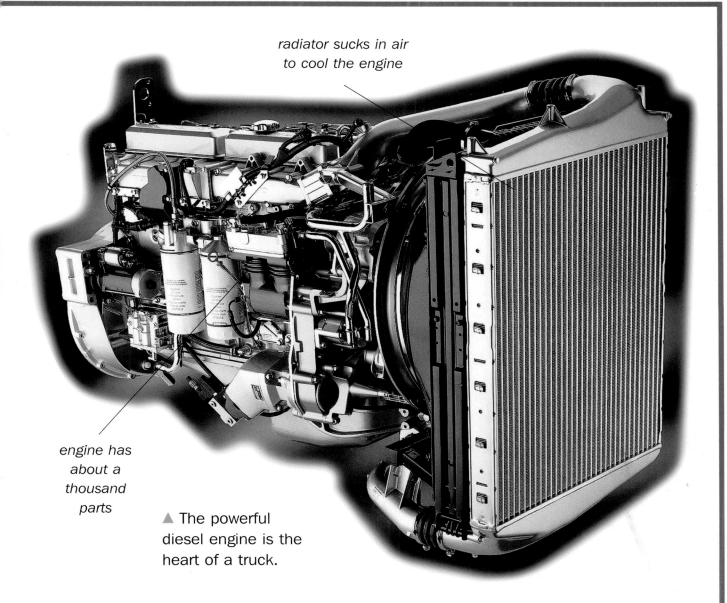

radiator sucks in air
to cool the engine

engine has
about a
thousand
parts

▲ The powerful
diesel engine is the
heart of a truck.

Usually the engine is hidden below a truck's cab. The picture here shows a new engine, before it goes into a truck.

The diesel engine is a complex piece of equipment, but it is tough and hard wearing. Most diesels give many years of reliable service.

⚙ **MOON TRUCKING**

A working truck may cover 800 000 km or more before being scrapped. This is about the same distance as driving to the Moon and back! Many parts in both engine and truck will be repaired or replaced during this time, from the tyres to the windscreen wipers.

BIG RIGS

Big rig is the nickname for the huge trucks that speed along the world's major highways.

▲ This rig can cruise at 120 km/h, where speed limits allow.

▼ A bug-screen at the front of this rig helps keep the windscreen free of insects.

bug screen

KENWORTH

R·8037

fuel tank at either side

'New trucks are designed with safety in mind. We set up a test truck to hit a concrete block at speed. The results are checked to make sure the safety equipment works. A dummy driver sits in the cab... The noise when the truck hits the block is *unbelievable!*'
Technician at test area

▲ New trucks have squashy air bags in the cab that protect drivers in a crash.

semi-trailer, or the load-carrying part of the rig

A big rig's rear section is called a semi-trailer. It hooks on to the back of the tractor. The semi can be unhooked at the end of a trip, to be unloaded. The trucker can quickly attach a newly-filled semi. This saves time, as the load can be driven away at once.

All sorts of things are hauled by truck. The rig pictured on the left is carrying fresh fish. These are kept cold by a refrigerator. Such cooling equipment is essential for loads that will spoil if they get warm – without it, this truck's fish would soon begin to smell.

LONG-DISTANCE TRUCKING

Many big-rig truckers cover a distance of 160 000 km a year. For truckers, this is just part of the job.

▲ This trucker takes a break on a long haul in Arizona, USA.

On long runs many truckers use sleeper cabs. If they use their rig as a mobile home, thieves cannot steal the truck or its load in the night. Sleeper rigs can be very comfortable. Bunk bed, clothes cupboard, hi-fi and microwave cooker are among the many things that can be fitted.

► The Kenworth T2000 sleeper cab is like a small caravan.

👁 TAKING A BREAK

'My sleeper cab may be compact but, in many ways, it's cosier than my real home! I have a small fridge for food, and a microwave reheats ready-meals quickly. I can watch colour TV and I have a paperback mini-library. I use the mobile phone to call my wife and children. Sometimes I play games on my laptop computer to relax before going to sleep – my favourite is a flight-simulator game. Maybe I should have been a fighter-jet pilot!' *Long-distance trucker*

▶ Truck cabs are filled with controls. Air-conditioning is used to keep the cab cool.

gauge shows engine speed

power steering system makes turning the wheel lighter and easier

A road train crossing the Outback is quite a sight. You can see dust thrown up by the wheels from kilometres away. If you are near the truck as it hurtles by, you can be choked by a mini dust storm. It's best to stay clear.

Kangaroos should keep away, too. Many are killed because they do not hop aside.

many kangaroos are hit by speeding trucks

parked semi-trailers

⚙ MELTING TYRES

It is so hot in the deserts of Australia's 'red centre' that truckers have to keep their speed down, so that the tyres don't melt. At noon, temperatures may be more than 40°C, so truckers drive at about 70 km/h. At night, when it is cooler, trucks can go faster.

TANKERS

▲ This tanker carries oil. The driver has to take great care, because oil can easily catch fire.

Tanker trucks haul many kinds of liquid. Some liquids are easy to carry, others need special care.

Liquids such as milk or water are easy to carry. They pour well, and can easily be pumped in and out of a tanker. Fats have to be heated, as they become solid when cold. Very cold liquids are kept cool with powerful refrigerators.

▲ It takes only a few minutes to pump 1000 litres of oil.

▶ This liquid oxygen tanker stores its load at a super-chilly -183°C.

⚙ SLOSHING ABOUT

No trucker wants a shifting load. This affects a truck's balance, making turning corners dangerous. To help, tank-makers build in 'anti-slosh' paddles. These are stiff metal blades inside the tank that slow down liquid when it swirls around. Tanks often have several small compartments, as sloshing in each of these is less than in one big tank.

▶ Ready-mixed concrete has to be kept turning so that it does not set hard before it arrives at a building site.

tanker body is made of special material to help keep the load cold

15

SHIFTING THE DIRT

The building industry uses trucks to haul away muck before the building work begins.

Dumper trucks are among the most useful heavy trucks. They have huge tyres and are super-strong. This means that they can take the knocks and bangs of tough work. Bigger trucks are often made of solid steel 25 mm thick.

Builders usually have to work in a hurry, so speed is important – for all its size, a dumper like the one below can roar along at 50 km/h or more.

▲ This dumper truck can carry 20 tonnes of dirt at a time.

► A dumper is loaded by a digger-excavator.

power shovel loads
three tonnes of rock
at a time

power-assisted
controls make
the excavator
easy to handle

⚙ DUCKWALKING DUMPER

This dumper is a 'frame-steer' design. It has a joint behind the cab. This lets the driver steer by twisting the entire front half of the truck from side to side, rather than just turning the front wheels. At slow speeds, frame-steer dumpers wriggle as they steer. Drivers call it duck-walking!

MEGATRUCK!

The world's heaviest trucks are used in the mining industry, for carrying huge loads of rock and earth.

Home for these mammoth trucks is in such places as the huge copper mines of Zaire, in Africa. Here, dumpers are driven round the clock, each one shifting thousands of tonnes of rock every day.

The biggest dumper of all is the Caterpillar Model 797. Fully loaded, the big Cat weighs about 600 tonnes, more than half of which is a huge mound of dirt, weighing about the same as a pile of 300 cars.

It may be big, but the 797 is easy to drive, because the controls are power-assisted.

▲ The Cat 797 can speed along at 64 km/h.

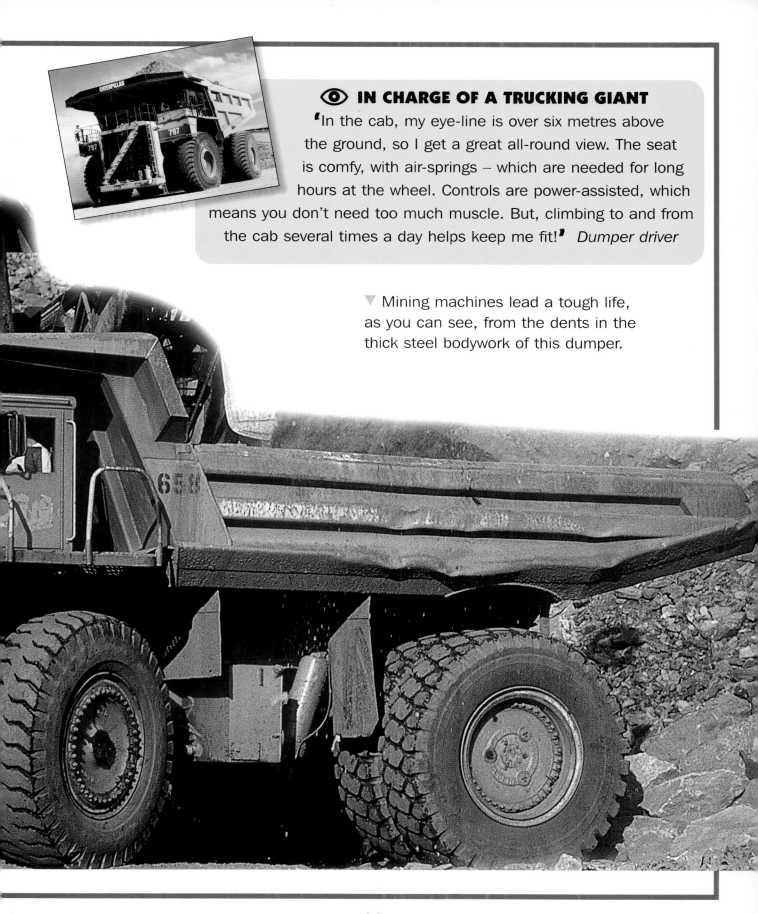

👁 IN CHARGE OF A TRUCKING GIANT

'In the cab, my eye-line is over six metres above the ground, so I get a great all-round view. The seat is comfy, with air-springs – which are needed for long hours at the wheel. Controls are power-assisted, which means you don't need too much muscle. But, climbing to and from the cab several times a day helps keep me fit!' *Dumper driver*

▼ Mining machines lead a tough life, as you can see, from the dents in the thick steel bodywork of this dumper.

FIRE FIGHTERS

Fire trucks range from pumpers, built to drench a fire, to extending-ladder trucks.

▲ The 1899 Merryweather fire engine used a steam engine for pumping water.

For fires in buildings, fire crews pump thousands of litres of water to drown flames. Once the fire is under control, dry powder can be sprayed on areas that are still hot.

In an aircraft or vehicle crash, burning fuel is the main danger. Here, fire crews spray foam at the fire. Water in the foam cools things down, and special gas in the bubbles smothers the flames.

▶ A ladder truck arrives at a blaze. The crew will soon raise the ladder to reach the fire.

fire-fighting platform

✿ UP ON A LADDER

Fire-fighters often have to reach the upper floors of buildings, where people might be trapped in a blaze. The extending ladder on this fire truck has a top platform to make rescues easier. There are movement controls on the platform, as well as down on the truck.

▶ Fire crews have to train so they are ready for any emergency. Here, an airfield crash truck sprays foam on an old airliner, used for practice.

foam is pumped on to fire

ladder can be raised and turned on truck's turntable

AN JOSE FIRE DEPT.

BREATHING AIR

LIGHT TRUCKS

Light trucks are very popular. They are chunky looking, and can carry big loads when needed.

Radio-controlled monster trucks are popular with many model builders. This one is 30 cm long.

Many light trucks have a four-wheel drive system, in which power from the engine goes to all the wheels. Four-wheel drive is useful for driving across rough country or in slippery mud. With all four wheels turning, you can keep going in places where a two-wheel drive truck would get stuck.

◄ This pick-up truck has a four wheel drive system.

⚙ DRIVING THE WHEELS

In most trucks – and cars – the engine drives two wheels, either at the back or the front. On a slippery surface, it's easy for these two wheels to lose grip so that they just spin round and round, and the vehicle stops. Four wheel drive adds a pair of powered wheels to give extra grip.

► The Hummer was first built as an army truck. Lots of pop stars and movie actors wanted one, so the maker made a version for them, too.

▲ Pick-up trucks with giant tyres and big engines perform as 'Monster Trucks' at shows. Often they crush cars as a favourite act!

engine is above the water line

FUTURE TRUCKS

Designers are busy working on trucks that will create little pollution and use less fuel. Making trucks quieter and safer is important, too.

Oily black diesel exhaust fumes could soon be a thing of the past. New engines burn their fuel better, so are cleaner than mucky old designs.

Natural gas is another kind of fuel. It is already used by some trucks. It burns very cleanly, so is especially good for trucks that are going to be used in cities.

▲ This present-day truck runs on natural gas. This is a fuel that creates much less pollution when burnt than diesel oil.

▶ This is one idea for a future truck. The body panels would be made of aluminium, a metal that does not rust.

⚙ BURNING NEW FUELS

Diesel oil is the standard truck fuel, and is likely to remain so, at least for the time being. Present-day diesels are cleaner than old types, and future designs will be even better. In the future, more trucks may use natural gas, which is cleaner than any diesel being planned. Hydrogen gas may also be used. Its waste gas is just steam, made of pure water.

◀ Designers still sketch out ideas on paper. This side view sketch shows how new, small, efficient engines may fit neatly into the chassis of a truck.

engine

wheel

▲ New designs are often shown off at truck races.

lightweight aluminium and plastic body – lighter trucks use less fuel

▼ Cugnot's steam truck, towing a cannon.

TRUCK FACTS

Here are some facts from the world of trucks and trucking.

Steam truck

The first truck was made by Nicholas Cugnot, in 1769. The steam-powered three-wheeler was built to haul guns for the French Army. A second model was built, and this could pull a four-tonne load, but only at walking pace.

Bulldog strength

The Mack company's trucks were called 'bulldogs' by soldiers for their strength and reliability in the army. Mack adopted the bulldog as its company symbol.

Mountain crossing

Truckers risk their lives when driving through the Himalaya mountains, between India and China. The roads are so bad that drivers often have to creep slowly along narrow tracks that wind along the sides of mountains. In the valleys far below lie the rusting wrecks of trucks that didn't stay on the road.

Saving fuel

A big rig uses about one litre of fuel every 3 km. Fuel costs money, so drivers use every trick they know to make savings. Even parking on a flat road to avoid an uphill start makes a small difference.

Computer truck

The Renault Magnum has a built-in electronic 'doctor', which checks on how the truck is performing. You can plug in a laptop computer to see the fuel used or distance travelled.

◀ Mack trucks have a shiny bulldog above the radiator grille.

Non-stop dumper

Giant mining dumpers are worked far harder than their drivers. Most dumpers are used 16 hours a day, with three or four changes of driver during that time. One record-breaking dumper beat this by working over 56 minutes an hour, every single day, for a year. The only time out was for refuelling and for servicing.

Race to the Clouds

Every year truckers roar up the 4343-metre-high Pikes Peak in Colorado, US, in a race to be quickest to the top. Back in 1901, when Pikes Peak racing started, it took over nine hours to get up. Today cars manage the run in just 10 minutes, and trucks are not far behind. The 1999 trucking king was Mike Ryan, who blasted to the top in just over 15 minutes. Ryan is actually a stunt driver – in the same year he jumped a truck over 20 metres through the air, while it was on fire!

▲ Dumper truck used for hauling rock from a mine.

Tachograph time

European drivers have a 'spy' in the cab called a tachograph. This notes time and distance travelled. The tacho is a safety device, made to stop truckers driving too long at a time. A tired driver can easily make a mistake and perhaps cause an accident.

Custom trucks

Customizing is a popular way to mark out your truck from others. Some people just add a name to the cab door, or maybe a stripe or two. Others go further, with gleaming new paint, chromed parts, leather seats and sleeper cabs with luxury fittings.

Muddy drive

In 1999, truckers taking food aid to refugees in Albania had to use roads that were often just long mud holes. At times it took an hour to slither along a five-kilometre stretch.

▼ Customized show truck.

TRUCK WORDS

Here are some of the technical terms used in this book.

▲ Cabover truck.

Air bag
A safety device stored inside the centre of a steering wheel. In a crash, it blows up almost instantly, to act as a cushion to protect the driver. Some trucks have a second air bag to protect a passenger.

Articulated
See rigid.

Big rig
The name for the combination of tractor and semi-trailer used for hauling big loads.

Cabover
A truck design that sits the cab on top of the engine. The cab tilts over so an engineer can reach the engine when it needs servicing. A conventional truck design has the engine under a long hood or bonnet in front of the driver.

Chassis
The strong metal structure to which truck parts (such as engine and wheels) are attached. The word is pronounced 'sha-see'.

Diesel engine
The type of engine used in most trucks. Invented by the German, Otto Diesel, in the 19th century. It burns special oil, and is efficient, though often quite noisy, compared to a petrol engine.

Four-wheel drive
Vehicle with engine power that drives all four wheels. In 'wheel code' this is known as a 4x4.

Frame-steer
An articulated truck that is steered by twisting the tractor unit from side to

Inside a diesel engine

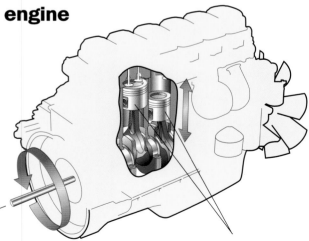

shaft turns wheels

pistons sliding up and down inside cylinders turn a shaft

28

side, rather than steering with the front wheels. These wheels roll forward or back, but do not change direction for steering.

Rigid

A truck with a single steel chassis, on which the cab and load area are mounted. Articulated ('artic') trucks are split into two sections, with the tractor in front. This pulls the load-carrying sections.

Road train

A big Australian rig, often with three or more trailers. Road trains haul loads across the vast outback, Australia's hot desert centre.

Semi-trailer

A type of trailer used with artic rigs. It can be hitched

▲ A mobile digger loads a rigid-chassis dumper truck.

and unhitched to a tractor in a few minutes. When unhitched, metal legs drop down at the front, to keep the trailer level.

Sleeper cab

A cab with its own built-in sleeping area. Most have a bunk bed, a small wardrobe, a TV and other comforts.

Tachograph

A machine fitted to European trucks. It shows the time and distance travelled. Drivers in tacho-equipped trucks must take breaks at set times, to avoid tiredness.

◀ The arrow shows one of this tanker semi's front support legs.

TRUCK PROJECTS

These easy experiments show you some of the science behind the world of trucks and trucking.

BENDING ROUND CORNERS

Articulated trucks are used for a very good reason – they are much easier to drive round tight corners. Try parking a model truck to see the difference having a separate truck and trailer makes.

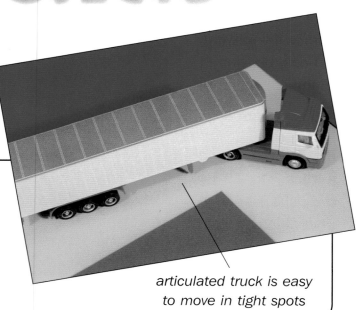

articulated truck is easy to move in tight spots

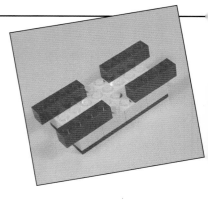

SPREADING THE WEIGHT

Big trucks have many wheels, to avoid sinking into soft ground, or breaking highway surfaces. For this experiment you need flour, a container, construction bricks and a 400 or 500g tin of beans.

1 Pour the flour into the container. You need a depth of about 30 mm. Level the surface with a flat-edged kitchen utensil, such as a plastic spatula.

2 Next, build a simple lorry shape from building bricks. Use a platform section, with two narrow bricks at each end. These do the job of wheels.

cooler fitted on front of trailer

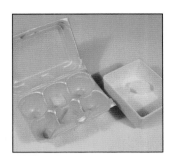

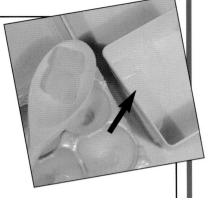

KEEPING LOADS COOL

Refrigeration units can keep a load cool, but good insulation is needed too, to help the cooling system. For this experiment you need a plastic egg box, a small container and four ice cubes. Time your experiment with an accurate watch.

1 Place two ice cubes in the egg box, then close it. Place two more ice cubes in the open container. Keep a note of the time.

2 After 20 minutes, the open ice cubes (arrowed) should be melting. Now check in the egg box. The cubes here should still be frozen.

3 Build a second unit, but have double-width bricks at the ends. This double-width should do the same job as the extra tyres on a full-size truck.

4 Place the first brick unit on the flour. Gently place the bean tin on top. Be ready to catch the tin if it falls sideways. When the bricks have sunk in, carefully lift the tin off and place to one side. Gently lift the brick unit out of the flour.

5 Measure how far the bricks have sunk in. Now smooth the flour and repeat with the double-width bricks. You should find this unit hardly sinks in at all.

INDEX